HEMISPHERE OF LOVE

Cyril Dabydeen

We acknowledge the support of the Canada Council for the Arts for our publishing program. We also acknowledge support from the Ontario Arts Council.

Cover design by Michael Crusz

National Library of Canada Cataloguing in Publication

Dabydeen, Cyril, 1945-
        Hemisphere of love / Cyril Dabydeen.

Poems.
ISBN 1-894770-12-9

        I. Title.

PS8557.A25H45 2003   C811'.54   C2003-903370-8
PR9199.3.D2H45 2003

Printed in Canada by Coach House Printing

TSAR Publications
P. O. Box 6996, Station A
Toronto, Ontario M5W 1X7
Canada

www.tsarbooks.com

To have a vision is not to see something that is not there,
but rather to see what is always there.

SHARON BUTALA, *Stone Heart*

Every moment contains the monumental and the ordinary.
BEN OKRI

CONTENTS

HEMISPHERE OF LOVE

BEING

HERE

WHAT WE ALWAYS KNOW

I have talked to the stones, pebbles,
the bear sniffing and walking
across a narrow river in a long journey,
as I've come to this understanding
in the middle of the forest floor
with pine and birch, the spruce
making the ground waver.

It is all we will ever hear about,
my hand cupping water, the tongue's
slaking of thirst because of the sun,
everything being close to my eyelids,
overwhelmed as I am once again . . .
and must leave well alone at night.

How else do we live if not with the impulse
to change, redrawing the maps because
of their original formation—
topography being finite above all else.

Now making amends with you
with shadows forming from large trees,
or bending in the wind, as a tornado too
we must come to grips with.

The bear is more than imaginary,
still walking along, drying itself with
a quiver and shake—
always with an unwelcome surprise,
as I look back at you, expecting
other journeys to begin . . .
          without making a false stride.

THE WALK

i
I have come to this understanding
that the lake is the greatest thing
in the mirror of silence as I try to bring
everything closer to pine and maple,
to shine anew with tundra, or to listen
to the loon's cry at this time of the year.

The partridge scuttles across thick brush,
as the lone Ojibwa boy runs after it . . .
while I conjure up other places—
ritual I am now more accustomed to.

Nanabijou, the Sleeping Giant, I talk to next
close to Mount McKay with origins in my mind;
or it's Slave Lake not far from Yellowknife
where Doctor Bud assisted with the delivery
of a child as the husband ate bits of moose
hanging from a wall. Later the wife sent
the Doctor a smelly mocassin, three months after.

ii
I again contemplate Lake Superior's silence,
because spruce trees keep hanging in water
forming shadows, always silhouetted with
other vegetation; other elements too, all
akin to one's tropical instincts still intact.

I make amends with a special longing as
ice-breakers move to the mouth of the lake
close to the marina where I'd painted that summer;
and it's still a surprise being in Thunder Bay
trying to understand why ripples come closer.
Birds' feet disappear in thick grass or moss,

as I consider other movements in this North:
this place which I don't easily forget, as impressions
keep me tied to solid ground or lush tundra.

iii
The land yet grows bigger, all in the lake's
formidable silence akin to being a miracle;
other emblems too bring the terrain closer
as I keep watching the rainbow at bay, or
Try making a name for myself because I keep
hearing wild horses running around at night,
or their just rearing up to go in blustery weather
as the imagination compels me to enact.

OLD TOWN
(*Yellowknife, NWT*)

From distance it's the beginning or shape of things
        not far from Great Slave Lake;
and Jackfish Lake is what I recall
or reminisce about as this town's beginning,
        or a place of government too it is,
yet mining gold and diamond on rocky terrain
        seem all with little else happening in Old Town.

The water's gentle waves with sea planes overhead:
a harbor without distress I take in, not far
        from Ragged Ass Road. And indeed
Wild Cat Café's now rundown, yet it's still
an original frontier, or just a small-scale Cabbagetown
says the taxi driver, who figures we are from
        out of town, or only from Toronto.

At the Arctic Art Gallery I buy an Inuit painting;
and the wind blows hard outside,
         the cold gleam of sunlight across the lake
I consider long; and the Dene and other native tribes
         who first lived here: copper knives . . .
or gold being still on their minds.
Caribou meat in a strip I chew,
         the locals telling me about real winter,
how awfully cold it gets up here,
         but they don't mind it—
it's a time for hibernation, you see.
In spring and summer outdoor activities
         are all they look forward to
 . . . camping, boating,
                  what else?

Here 35-degree below weather stays for a long time,
and Mayor Lovell, who'd visited the Amazon,
who once hankered after a life in Brazil,
         then moved north, and has since lived here
for near forty years—
                  says he really loves it!

The Dog Rib Indians now begin to dance
for visitors like me who still think of the tropics,
         and someone calmly says Natives aren't used
to the word "music," yet every group
         has its own drums: "It's our people's distinct ways,"
with rhythm all around—
         and we must come here again

Maybe not unlike the Japanese tourists—
         the three thousand who come each year,
from Osaka, all wanting to see the aurora borealis,
         the spectacular Northern Lights,
though some will fall easily on the ice, the snow
         compelling them to slippery ground.

6

Indeed the trees never grow tall here: they're lollipops,
says Toronto City Councillor Howard Moscoe
as he holds on to an Inuit sculpture he bought,
    while I contemplate the Heritage Building
or the Franklin Expedition, eager to find my own
    Northwest Passage to what's called the Orient . . .
and John Franklin was a stalwart, I say, recalling
Earlier that day meeting the world-champion
    sled-dog team racer (Chipewyan): a name
I quickly scribbled down on a piece of paper,
    hoping for excitement with words,
or being amazed at how really vast Canada is.

    Other places in my mind's eye,
as I plan to visit here again, despite weather being
    permanent on a postcard, with rainforests
yet on my mind, or distant voices calling louder
    like my own familiar spirit, more than mayors
or other politicians will ever understand—
    no matter where they come from,
or just pretend we're all one on this vast land.

(September 6, 1997)

ON SHEDIAC BEACH

Dead as stone the crab, pecan coloured,
or what seems like ordinary rust now
as three women and I contemplate time
at the ocean's edge here in New Brunswick.

With a tourist's eye mindful of custom,
we're independent in our wandering way
with a beating vulnerability of the senses
as the crab is unearthed, and it no longer scuttles

Yet seems ready to avert a seagull's gaze.
A few yards away a girl digs holes in the sand,
searching for clams; and it's now our intrusion
against her determined ways I come to understand.

A tryst it is, our spirit being one with hers:
this girl still oblivious of us, being bent on
observing the crab, or simply measuring
the ocean like foreign ground before us:
Fissures of sand, as all things seem beached down
here, and will come to an end before long,
as the women quietly drift away. I hail
to them as they take in two men like humps

In the distance in the water ahead; and one male
waves back because of our attempts to bring worlds
together with everything soon becoming billows.
I reach down to my knees, indeed making eye contact

With the dead crab lost for all time: the curve of shell,
or it being mere crustacean here at the limits of the sea;
prehistoric too it is, with clams dug up, or what seems
forever lost but will soon be found alive again.

(September 10, 1995)

·SHOVELLING SNOW
(*a Nova Scotia journal*)

Shovelling snow is like shovelling dreams,
who we are or will become—
as I listen to the pregnant woman
talk about the lack of respect for her
(meaning self-respect), who understood that
at Cherrybrook the Baptist church continues
long, while Micmac Rita Joe again sings
        praises about her people.

And Carrie Best is still at it, who knows?
more underground crossings, another train's
journey in the making; and the Mohawk next
talks about the lack of self-respect being due
to nothing but self-hate—
        there's no halfway point.

Where solitudes yet prevail, I sing
in the church choir without raising
my voice, hallelujahs here in the Halifax Counties;
and Mayor Wallace, a former middleweight boxing
champion, weighs in, as we are once more
at the Black Cultural Centre with Henry Bishop,
and Wayne Adams still with politics in his veins.

Doc Savage—a Welshman, former mayor of Dartmouth,
then Premier—strong on housing and welfare payment
I also tell about, with a promise of something better;
and I've grown to accept race or ethnic origins
like a clot of blood because of where I've come from.

I face up to the odds of living in a new country
and indeed sing praises to Empire Loyalists,
shovelling snow because settlements still carry
footprints of those who have been here longest—
all that I will know about in days to come.

ON A CALM DAY

Places that begin with concatenation,
distances in the cock-crowing hour,
or it being mere flirtation in the wind.

An entire sea or ocean, this criss-crossing
boundaries and showing up in strange places
as I drift like a wayward flotilla it seems.

Attracted to other regions along the way,
I pretend to like hibiscus, zinnia, or other
flora that appear long on the horizon.

Palm groves come closer as waves appear
in the mind's eye like odd shapes while
I begin to wonder where it will all end.

A desert opens miraculously too, and I'm
at a loss for words because clay tablets will
tumble down and yet become pebbles, dust.

The low ground is again mountainous
as a pyramid rises high or seems etched
against the sky while poets gnash their teeth,

Compelled to discover other worlds, or simply
long to create what the imagination forbids:
water pouring out, trees growing in an oasis,
All in a new state, as architects breathe hard,
and I lie fitfully on the ground here in the far
north and now seem to start spinning around.

AN ALBUM

I've decided living in Ontario
is the best thing for me,
the weather being normal
as I contemplate ease.

I listen to the elevator
like a trap door moving up
and down without an echo:
all civilizations have ways

of ending up in America,
maybe, as I try to understand
more about meeting places:
history being beyond reprieve;

or a mere disaster one after
another, according to the man
who boasted about exploitation
ike his religious creed—

who's still considered a hero, he says.
Quietly I defy other claims
like stone tablets, a burning
fire being all I can bear now

from a mountain top—
locusts yet overpowering me
as I continue to rely
on the Old Testament,

or try to be braver than Daniel
in an irksome lion's den,
or just being the son of Abel—
my own father no less;

and the one woman who'd
come under his spell
in a place distant now, I recall,
and inhale tropical airs.

or simply consider life
being a throwback—
all where I've come from
like other states of being,

as I talk myself hoarse
with claims of a new country,
or it's the sheer desire . . .
to live life independently.

UPPER CANADA VILLAGE

1

Nothing takes us by surprise,
but a time of long ago
transplanted to Morrisburg
as I view history with a cannon
here at my young daughter's side.

She holds her own against enemies
across the river or lake; and a train
comes along without fanfare
while I try to understand history
more than Upper Canada Village.

2

I make my mark with sightseeing,
never being distant from Ottawa
or Kingston, places I have conquered
in my style, as I begin to climb uphill—
now with one solid step at a time,
facing enemies unknown in frontier style.

She will carry on from where I've
left off because of days gone by—
those wearing uniform in her mind,
always like false attire no doubt.

And it's because of what's yet to come,
facing enemies always greater,
as cannons always fire louder
because of words we sometimes string out
to register who came here first,
which the young will be asked to remember.

IN HEAVY WEATHER

The city's ground
Or landscape,
I follow

Without pretence,
Here in the Great
White North

You say,
Sinking
To the bottom

Smelt-fishing
Now in the Kaministikwa
River

Floating birch
Before me, Huck Finn
Again, a further

River, thud-thudding
In a logging camp,
A woodpecker's Jim

Is all I remember,
Being moose too
And tramping—

In heavy weather

IN THE CREEK

In the creek, the shallowness of water . . .
always murky brown
with floating vegetation—
all things that must go under
in this the darkest time of the year:

Water swirls, eddying—
voices of ancestry . . .
mermaids singing, too,
somewhere because of what I hear.

Seashells, other vegetation: water hyacinths
& seaweed; a dead cow floating with
a long-billed crane on its back being
 contemplative in the current's own style.

A chameleon basks in the sun
with fits of greenery, I note;
and this one bird is dead still
watching the horizon with clouds
coming down, indeed.

The creek meanders, forming shapes:
pebbles, stones, or just one large boulder;
the tall trees around being like a miracle,
this moment when the one bird
suddenly takes off,
And remains solid in the air!

GATINEAU HILLS

Outside, flocking like so much sheep,
Ba-baaing silence with snowdrifts at the bend.

More wetness on the ground, cold, cold—
Suddenly with a strong wind at my feet,

Heels darting. Turning once again,
With more speed, and moving swiftly

From tree to tree in this make-believe
That there's less danger lurking

At an angle. The body leaning forward,
Something greater than a frown; the sun

Next, the heart's own sudden velocity,
Pounding with a drive against the wind.

Blood overwhelming all else, throbbing
Through the darkness, whitely—

Sheep's down.

BEING HERE

Being here, where else? Instincts buttressed
with memory as I balk at the new place.

I say, Wait awhile as I travel on another
journey while the ocean's still full.

I throb at the limits, if you must know,
and remember other emblems.

At the river's mouth there are openings:
this living world without a sense of valour

Or make-believe as the waves rise higher.
Sounds of a siren too after regular hours,

The conch shell presaging what's to come:
seaweed or other forms of sargasso,

Like the Atlantic's own distress signals,
as I again come forward with crossings

Still holding the oars aloft.

HORSES IN THE DARK
(for Timothy Findley)

This instinct compelling us to believe—
mementoes of shapes as we dwell on
more than memory; hoof beats all around,
the ground overwhelming us at a glance.

The light's dazzling speed with bat or owl;
other creatures that we call our own
and are not as we inhale the stale air,
the sea at our command like a further miracle.

We genuflect with the sun coming down,
the trees spreadeagling shadows . . .
the leaves' own choir in variegated music,
as the horses lunge forward with trajectory

Or circular movement; arabesques, shadows without
the sense of oblivion because of hopes we cherish,
being finally here as the ground seeps in;
now the anxieties of our age with offsprings

Watching us as we try to redeem ourselves,
contemplating aspirations with other rhythms
keeping us honed in: emotions paralyzing us
because of who we are. The horses go round and round,

Heads raised, fire coming from their nostrils—
they attempt to leap off the ground, Pegasus-like;
instincts we now know are too precious
for us to make much use of, the light startling us

With a speed we never thought previously possible.

SURRENDER

There are places in our midst
akin to larger rivers,
          or a vast terrain—
     we will continue to traverse.

All you have encountered
          more than Epictetus
or other destitutes in ancient places . . .

Now I wander with crossings,
   more than the Greeks ever did,
this beginning of new life—
     without the sense of history.

Conquest at the fingertips,
          spires raised higher,
as if there's joy in stars moving.
An ocean brings us together
          with tides, as I look back at houses
on stilts, being one with another.

FAR FROM AFRICA

She walks down the busy street,
as this man with parcels weighing
down his arms accosts her;
a new immigrant from Africa,
he's here now in Ottawa.

Irish to the core, she's Belfast born,
you bet; attended Alexandra College
in Dublin, went to school with
W B Yeats's granddaughter—
she holds her head up high.

He comes after her:
Can you scratch my nose,
please? Words mutely said.
It isn't a come-on.
Then what?

She fled, as he's left standing there,
weighed down with his parcels,
itching still, or being forlorn
because of where he comes from,
Africa . . . time's behest.

SELF-KNOWLEDGE

The man just back from the South Pacific,
a place far in-between,
who once imagined himself superior,
but has now come to understand life better
after living five years among people
        different from himself.

His own ways he now appreciates best
because he will never forget that
in the heat of Papua New Guinea
people move at a different pace;
and the elder who'd said to him:
        "Never mistake knowledge
for wisdom; one helps you make a life;
the other helps you live a life."

It's like walking in someone else's moccasin
and developing intimate self-knowledge,
which he must daily come to grips with.

BEAUTY
OF
T O E S

THE BEAUTY OF TOES

i

The beauty of toes
on soft ground,
far from the illimitable sky;
the soil topsy-turvy,
the curvature of flesh
or splinters of wood
as we look down from above:
who we are, how many fingers
we have left, how many toes,
this exchange with antlers
or simply make-believe.

Nails growing on one hand,
horns becoming extremities
as we're still on circular ground;
and it takes seventy years
or more before things begin
to wither and die,
the heart palpitating,
the lungs giving out
                    in a *whoosh!*

Breath of air really,
grasping at things, then moving
from tree to tree for a better view;
even being a sloth of sorts,
hanging with one arm—
the liana bent I'm sure.

ii

Here a white-watered terrain
close to the Zambezi and the Nile,
the Brahmaputra making us believe

all rivers are one long vein;
the Ganges and St Lawrence too,
if you must know; then . . .
the Orinoco and the Amazon—
at this juncture.
      I walk barefooted,
my toes' indelible imprint
on delta, topsoil, the terrain
of wood and plaster,
because of who I am—
or we all are.

Nurturing false hopes, dreams
also putative, as we are here
to stay, believe me.
Pyramids of lost time, an obelisk
sun scorching as the toes
keep making us go on to places,
or leaving us at the desert limits.

Indeed the Pharoahs have carved nothing,
hands clawing for more space
in a tomb or mausoleum,
the noise of tourists being all,
my counting to ten in Arabic . . .
what Ptolemy or young Tutenkhamun
have said, always with portents:
signs coming down through the ages,
I must consider or actually believe in.

The graven image, my offering
prayers to stranger gods,
Ra no less, because of the magic
of numbers; or a cat carved
with a self-styled grimace
that I remember.

iii

With Copernicus I continue to think
of the round earth differently,
the sun's position always changing;
the toes becoming gnarled
without perfection: closer to the heart,
lungs, face . . . eyes . . . ears . . . lips.
Indeed I have scores to settle,
over vast areas of topsoil:
with the jay bird and crow,
or being a desert albatross,
or a condor in South America—
the toes bringing me here, and
I cry out with the heart's
               authentic gasp.

At the Bronx Zoo or some place
where the silk-cotton tree bends,
forming a rainbow, I keep looking down—
toes ochre or sepia brown, registering
the tradition of webbed feet,
the ducks' own no less . . .
digging in, holding up myself
before becoming mudsplattered . . .
finally being on solid ground.

I make amends and keep wondering
who I am, and why there's really no
other place to go to: no other boundary
in the mind despite welcoming truths
about a far place in a wider universe.

The toes simply interchange
with fingers, lips, eyes, ears;
nostrils becoming flared,

bringing us to this realization
that we will live out our lives fully
without reconnoitering on topsoil.

The maple tree springing up,
as we move closer together,
my being too long in one place—
or remaining forever
        at a standstill.

HUMBLE AND FRIENDLY

To be humble and friendly among local gatherers
        in a yet dark continent; further travels in your mind
like an ongoing safari,
        you tell me with affection

All in the imagination's pulse,
        being never far from brush fires,
the horizon heating up
        before the mind's eye.

In a cold climate the moon keeps coming down
        with other landscapes. Time to outlast,
you say, remembering sitting among people you
        never truly understood

Because of territories too vast: humility being all,
        with the desire always
to map out territory—
        more than Karen Blixen ever did.

Now being *Out of Africa* without
        the commitment to make a name
        for yourself, I listen to you
tell again and again with a determined voice

In this downtown office; others listening
        to the images stored up—
which are never really far away
        from your self-styled dark continent.

FLIGHT

1
Flying into the Cheddi Jagan International Airport
in a moment of time with talk of love,
or a new destiny it seems like,
ceremonies beginning all over.

A further beating of the breast,
or imagining people in throes
because of where we've come from
with emblems close to the heart

Falsifying the ground as Arawaks and Caribs
look out without memory or pain;
only the curare of instincts, the arrow
bent into the shape of a rainbow.

2
I take stock of a country with all regions
as one from this Canada, this cold North,
or a journey with the sense of genesis,
so to speak, breathing in harder—
Making much ado of zinnia,
frangipani; the toucan staring back
with large eyes; a hummingbird doing
an acrobatic dance of its own

Above the eucalyptus; the stinking-toe
tree in a gust of trade wind.
Promises I keep to myself
as the races combine or simply mix.
All new states we now call a country:
one people with a destiny to uphold,
hopes we cherish because of timehri
shaped by crossings that I truly behold

While considering places my own,
the imagination's no less; strident voices
in me still echoing with time to outlast,
or what will never be the same again.

POINTE DES CHATEAUX, GUADELOUPE
(for Frantz and Dany Quillen)

Here at the tip of the Atlantic
   where the huge cross rises—
waves are also like islands
      coming forward—
         the bathers' rhythm
with surf lashing the rock's coral
   or volcanic formation.

   Walking along I consider
other islands, streets;
   an errant sea really,
bringing myself to you
   at a breakneck speed—
throwing myself in,
   a drowning once again—
      I hear you say.

My *Indianite's* presence
   with tremor of hands, knees,
heart throbbing, and walking
 step by step across the valley;
      ah, those details,
   in my bare-French words,
      or indentured forgetfulness.

The cross looms higher: magnificence,
   or watery death. Seas, oceans—
Mariama or the Holy Mary,
   journeys now at a standstill—
   my heritage or this tradition,
the body yet floating, hurling,
   into a larger place.
St Francois or Moule—
      coming to a heave and roll
with you at Pointe des Chateaux;
   the tourist yet in me—
brings us closer together.

   Now pointing to Maria Gallante's
majestic blue or aquamarine, the white surf's
   sail, bare breasted, beauty at the crest—
my heaving before an entire crowd's
   surge altogether in us—
         now reclaiming
islands.

                                   (December 15, 1990)

DECLARATION

This declaration of possibilities,
it is the way with metaphors,
weighing reforestation like antlers.

Such verbs,
this bush camp's sweat,
hewing out of solid wood

Or being up at five in the morning
and preparing to take
the woodpecker by surprise.

All sound without fury—
I am hardly at rest
at Trapper Lake
Believe it or not
as I am pigeonholed
a prairie poet by Revenue Canada.

I am prouder yet of my heritage
and those who came and listened,
the Lakehead scholars—

Who have eased the anger
out of me since the beginning—
now find me mellow

Like Suknaski's disdain
with harmonica strumming—
he being less Ukranian.

I succumb for a while—
this style is all
I am left with

Eager as I am to read on,
my dialect's best
even as I pretend.

LEGACY

Let me answer to the moon,
The pace set hard.

I breathe heavily
With fury on my tongue;

Oh, this test of thunder,
A lightning heartbeat again.

You, following from behind,
My other self, if you must know—

Shadowy footprints,
A mouth longing, rose dropping

Petals on dry grass.
I return to that place,

My home, country,
Land spinning

In my midst;
Nighttime really—

Overtaking
The moon's glimmer,

All the familiar paths
As I keep on

Being a patriot—
This hollow time . . .

Storing the winter
In my blood.

MULTICULTURALISM

I continue to sing of other loves,
Places . . . moments when I am furious,
When you are pale and I am strong
As we come one to another.

The ethnics at our door
Malingering with heritage,
My solid breath—like stones breaking.
At a railway station making much ado about much,
This boulder and Rocky Mountain,
CPR . . . heaving with a head tax
As I am Chinese in a crowd,
Japanese at the camps;
It is also World War II:
Panting, I am out of breath.

So I keep on talking
With blood coursing through my veins:
The heart's call for employment equity,
The rhapsody of police shootings in Toronto;
This gathering of the stars one by one,
Codifying them and calling them planets—
One country really . . .

Or galaxies of province after province,
A distinct society too—
Quebec or Newfoundland; the Territories . . .
How far we make a map out of our solitudes,
As we are still Europe, Asia,
Africa; and the Aborigine in me
Suggests love above all else—
The bear's configuration in the sky.
Other places, events; a turbanned RCMP,
These miracles–

My heritage and quest, heart throbbing,
Voices telling me how much I love you,
YOU LOVE ME; and we're always springing surprises,
Like vandalism at a Jewish cemetery,
Or Nelson Mandela's visit to Ottawa
As I raise a banner high on Parliament Hill—
Crying "Welcome!"—we are, you are . . .
OH CANADA!

ETHNICITY

You will not
tell
your ethnic ancestry

You will insist
that you are from
Toronto

Nevertheless—
and that this city
in which you are

A translator
is no different
from any other

Now that you are
lost
in the melting pot
Sad to say—
and whatever else
there is in you

Becomes less
permanent
as time goes by

A VISIT TO INDIA

1

A place I have never been to before,
but intrigued about since childhood.
Bihar or Mumbai, as the indenture spirit
is at a standstill: archives in me
as I make much ado about history,
or being a gymnast late at night with
images from The Royal Reader.
Tigers roaming, elephants marauding,
Shakuntala again pouring out with rain.

Where my ancestors have come from,
I pretend to acknowledge or not understand,
having denied other places from times past,
or living with lore of the Amazon instead:
evergreen forests bolstering a greenhouse
effect as environmentalists talk loudest.

2

Now in Ottawa in an Indian restaurant
with a Mexican name, the waitress takes in
Chandra Mohan, our Indian guest in authentic
attire, who mutters about Chairs of Canadian Studies
in India, or ways of making Canadian Literature
better known to a billion people there, all
in Delhi, Calcutta or Chennai, and where else?
Now James Reaney's an institution, he adds,
though he likes Margaret Atwood best.
So I ask, Why the interest in Canada?
Indeed it's about Rudy Weibe's Big Bear,
Robert Kroetsch's postmodernism,
or language-use in the Prairies, while I come
to grips with a tropical itch, being
foreign born and mulling over ways
of coping with identity in Canada.

3

Postcolonialism strides I contemplate
with Nehru's jewel-in-the-crown test or tryst
with destiny, Empire being what my forefathers took
less seriously while I'm here in the Great White North:
          a Susanna Moodie frontier in me,
as I claim to be a drawer of water and hewer
of wood, or dwell on a garrison state because
of the giant neighbour to the south,
          survival instincts merely—

Imagining continents that were once together,
as metaphors indeed make the world one;
and I again conjure up images like false truths,
reinstating Mowgli because of Kipling,
being astride an elephant and trundling along
in a jungle safari with mahout shouts,
blowing my horn because the British had been
          in India longest.

Now self-contained with aspirations
or a further quest, I think about what might
have been in Jaipur or Shimla, or some other place
unknown to me while yet being a maharajah
          in an exotic wilderness.

ON A LOCAL TRAIN IN MUMBAI
(*for Coomi Vevaina*)

After taking in Elephanta:
and the *trimurti*
     out on an island
on a sweltering hot day—
     I enter the train
in Mumbai with you, Parsi
scholar, and watch people
huddling,
     all trying to get in,
along with the many tourists.

     The crowd not defeated,
but with an accustomed ease
or frenzy due to their state
of poverty or what seems like it;
     and two young girls:
eight or nine, with eyes large
     as a cow's,
shabby clothes worn past their knees,
     unique in style.

And you say in India it's so special
     because of what
has to be learned,
     or endured
as a movie star handsome youth,
     determined at the back—
plays mournfully on his harmonium;
     the train moving along,
and he sings a bhajan,
     to establish the right mood.

The two girls take their
turn to ask for alms,
        coming to us next—
as I long to stand up
        and listen to the centuries unfolding;
the girls' eyes wider . . .
        as an entire continent
opens before me

        While across the Arabian Sea,
Elephanta's images still form,
the train chug-chugs along—
        and I record sensations
with affection or simple love
        I can never truly return.

(November 1, 1997)

SOUTH AMERICA

The day President Kennedy was shot,
I sat silently before the KB radio
listening desultorily to other worlds.
The boys outside in sparkling sunshine
excitedly played a game of cricket
near the jamun and black sage;
and Vaco, swarthy hued, imagining
being at the Oval or Lord's in London,
railed up, throwing the ball
hard down the pitch.
I watched him in a moment's puzzlement,
little as he could see of me because news
of the assassination was all.
Numbed, I sat before the radio
with requiem music playing,
the dirge that would remain long
and made much about
by local politicians.

Rage in our lives, with the yearning
to go north, Vaco most of all,
he yet lunging forward:
the ball pitched harder, as I kept
considering the life we lived
with stranger destinies ahead.

Years later with Dallas on my mind,
Lee Harvey Oswald being made
much about with his ties
to Cuba and Russia,
I became more perplexed;
by now Vaco had made his way
to America.

Not long after the news came
from Columbus, Ohio, of his
disappearance: the Vietnam War
having consumed him,
his death being because of drugs
or the military—
he never being much
with religion, I knew.

His mother and father, illiterate
and lost, kept yearning
for their missing son
with growing remembrance each year,
while I rehearse Kennedy's ongoing
assassination like my own private
sorrow all these years.

POLITICIAN
(*for Feroze*)

After a six-month sojourn,
you returned from Moscow
    with a copy of Mayakovsky's latest
beautifully bound (for me)

Rain clouds took on trousers;
I hoped for pickets of gold,
    while the censors appeared in dreams,
hounding him to his death

And the rain poured
as we talked about the art
    of redeeming a life . . .

A decade later you stood up
in Parliament and brought whole
    continents together

(APPLAUSE)

YOU, ANDREI VOZNESENSKY

I am less acquainted with formalism—
you, whispering about states of being,
Margaret Trudeau you wanted to know
about best, details registering in my mind.

The shape of alphabets like a curse,
hanging around your neck. Ah, do you
still think of the demise of socialism
and the palpitating death of the Soviet Union,
you, once nearly committing suicide?

Was Gorbachev really held captive for a while?
Was Yeltsin for the people at all cost?
Tell me from afar of people still needing bread;
and about Lenin, whom you might have once dreaded,
whose iron will impressed more than anything else,
and still lies in his mausoleum, and is no longer a threat.

This semblance of words and constructing new phrases,
like old-fashioned truths or too-easy improvisation—
creating out of the doldrums a new society . . .
With Yevtuskenko and the others, do you still champion
freedom in the new world order? Words have their own
ways of eking out virtues, as I pretend to hear.

And we talk again of how succinct language can be,
the tight lines the mind must come to grips with . . .
Mayakovsky still dreaming of pockets becoming rain clouds;
the voice or image you constantly hear about in the west,
hoping to show courage . . . and Lenin finally will rest in peace
with the metaphor of a casket . . . closed—
yet collectively put next to his mother's grave
with a distinct ceremony broadcast on CNN:
Where else?

ACORN'S THIRD WORLD

I give you Nicaragua
  and all the other places;
    I give them to you
where the sun shines naturally.
  I give you the hinterland forest
where jaguars snarl and leap
          from branch to branch
like playful kittens.
            I give you Grenada and all other
islands where sugar cane workers
          plod from day to day—
  bodies bent, gnarled,
            cane juice sticky on their arms,
legs, all day long.

  I give you all other places
in Central America
      where there's no calm . . .
Bolivian miners
        wheezing at nights,
still oppressed.
  I give you this domain of land,
    all of Canada—
from East to West Coast . . .
  Newfoundland not least,
        BC forest workers,
those in Northern Ontario mines—
          all who one day will unite,
as you said.

  Craggy faced as you were then,
    and I still wanted to nominate you
        Chairman of the League
of Canadian Poets, and to hear you,

Milton Acorn, sing loud
from your innermost veins
now that you are truly
at rest.

FOR ROLF HASENACK
—Dominican priest

The creak of old boards,
windows
rattling on a farm;
shingles moving in
every direction.

Power saws startle us
with jagged teeth,
and the trees
cry out vengeance.

With sawdust eyes
I long for new
place against foul
weather,

Thunder yet
another clarion call—
the rain being all;
in snow and wetness,
I give you a bunch
of wild flowers.

A builder too I am,
coming out
of dark caves,
scampering about
like mice.

The corpuscles
protest
the loss of dignity
at this vantage
point of roofs

Bedroom doors,
unreachable
as I am—
like castles,
palaces.

Together we watch concrete,
slabs of stone
genuflecting like
pious old men and women;

An anointing too
it is, for the homeless,
shelterless—
for how long?

Noting your anguish
with each creaking
board, and will
the sun only
keep us warm?

HEMISPHERE

OF

L O V E

ENTRIES

i

no window. this is no house. a rainshuttered day. open
spaces. savannah and territory. all worlds yet to come.
rivers. mountains. places we yearn to be in, will be . . .

our ancient ways swashbuckling or buccaneering. breathe
harder if you must. the night's watch, heaving once again.
listen, this too is a message of hope and survival.

somewhere afar, i hear you. memory's hovel, slave time . . .
what difference does it make? our identities carved, shaken
by indenture also . . . the aftercomers (so to speak). now the
arawak or carib in me. remembers-remembering. palpitating
breath, like fish on dry land. black sage and acacia still being all.

further boundaries in my midst, as i am here. nowhere else . . .
this talking to myself until hoarse. a creole's coconut-shelled
dream, resounding. still muttering at the sea's edge. tremors
beating at my wrist, my finless hand. other pulse beats, like
a tempest really. my lungs' own resuscitation. hear me!

ii

ochre and sepia brown. hyacinths also. remember, again that
river as i am moving to it with hope undiminished. i am still
here, in many places at once. i gather all the selves, mirroring
them at the continuing river's stretch. cane punts clanging,
beating, the earth resounding. a plantation's cauldron. again
a village, other voices in me with the disappearance of selves.
my meeting you at the zenith of another place. where we are,
or now must be in . . .

this great white north, i hear you say. cities also. i'm in the ruins
of parliament also, moving about without gunpowder. a clock
chimes, the peace tower only. you dare to come closer. then
surprises at skating down a canal, the longest in the world.

51

indeed, places that we are always going to. next champlain
meeting me eye to eye. a lumber town's lore. here . . . now a
place of embassies, high commissions. bureaucrats always
whispering behind closed doors. my own tongue's strength or
weakness . . . hear me . . . the spirit's own beginning, from
Macdonald to the present . . .

you, the cree, the iroquois, the ottawan. you, moving about
stealthily. a friendship centre in my veins also. you, nowhere,
 this canoe ride, somersaulting down or up river. tributaries
forming. an emblem of rockliffe park, terrain after terrain. my
sussex drive and colonel by, as we are still one.

this suzannah moodie in me also. being the last frontier. making
mockery, as i breathe harder one last time. i mutter and take it
all in stride . . . standing next to you . . . who am i . . . what must i
listen to, these stirrings of new adventure. or simply criss-crossing
terrain in time's quest . . . the close-up tropics, closer or afar . . .
my unending bush garden . . .

iii
day in, day out, blackwatered rivers. like further ruins. teeth
chattering in the cold wind. i move out from the concrete
planks of cities. my tongue still shrill as i move faster across
snowbanks, going farther north. again upriver. bass, pike, and
salmon in me. again the beaver . . . a dam's juncture. the world's
teeth bared at the edge of a log. i listen, this muskeg time really.

i am determined to stay here. freezing despite the hot sun's
memory . . . like further emblems. the igloo's own survival,
hunkered down. my being's presence, mingling with inner
furies or coming joyfully as one. now calling out the ethnic
names . . . newer places. snow's imprint further along the
highway. terry fox, i come with you, stepping along, the wind
in my face. you, nanabijou, old man's mountain. a rip van

winkle spirit with me, like no other time as i heave again and again, in much stronger wind.

the vanquished self i am, caught dead in my tracks. no longer going back to the past, or coming to the present. talking of new-ness and muttering a language of ice. fire. we who must be at peace on this ground-earth. the terrain fulfilling itself. sand and soil. springs. fountains. waves slapping against the shore. the water's own muttering, like droppings. time's own, i say, like a miracle . . . alas!

A GOAT IN THE YARD

Moments in the sun when all is perplexity—
the same ochreous shape with variation of tones
or determination with an old shoe, leather being
more than an affectation in the breeze.

The clouds somersault, and the bewildered goat
is without a sense of oblivion: on grass, sawdust,
empty shells, rotten boards, shingles, as I contemplate
an old shoe with a personality all its own.

The goat quickly moves forward, hooves scuffing the sun
without the sky's imprint as I also cherish hibiscus,
broken petals on glass, leaves on the ground, and
imagine Noah at the crossroads all at once.

A semblance of rutted soil, my now being held
to one spot as I'm about to start speaking in tongues
with a derelict stove, porcelain, potsherd, orchids
forming on buttressed roots setting the world afire.

A burning bush really, as I am thrust among
animals locking horns amidst the Hebrew flood;
the goat ruts hard from high ground, and
I look up with a sturdy glare, mesmerized

By the power an old shoe can muster. The goat
swaggers on blamelessly with a tufted beard,
amazed as I am at what else is transformed
with images through the ages, or never far away.

MANNERS
(for H&M)

My friend's manners never cease to amaze;
      he tells his young daughter
I suck my big toe when I sleep to rouse her fancy.

She's bound to remember such things
      that will make an older child blush.
He welcomes me with zest—

Says I hardly even kissed him,
      rests his case by insisting he's not shy,
has lost a good deal of his anger, naturally,

Now whatever is left of it, he adds,
      is used to good purpose.
I congratulate him on his manner;

      After nine years life must be different;
we talk about filling the gap of years
      with laughter.
Pain in his eyes, he still takes various
      members of a spreading family
by surprise. And when I leave
I imagine him making arresting turns
      on the Don Valley
Parkway as I detect a conspiracy of sorts

In his suggestion that friends must stick
      together, if only to make the children
remember what's long lost, or is yet to come.

MY MOTHER

i

I am doing it again:
I've fallen into the old trap,
telling my mother
she must forsake the old ways,
must go out in the snow
day or night and start jogging:

She who has lived most of her life
in the tropics, and toiled long,
raising her children, us;
suddenly I want her to be
in the fashion magazines,
to live with panache, be confident,
or overbearing in her dealings
       with people.

Never to be quiet anymore, as I tell her
to change her diet so as to lose weight,
even try to overcome stress,
exercise regularly: she must!
She balks, though never loudly,
and maybe she wants to do as I tell her—

I, her eldest, who's attended university,
who figures he knows it all—
indeed I know what's best for her
because I've been here longest
(so I believe).

Telling her again, as brothers and sisters
listen and say I'm too demanding—
yet I continue to berate her each time
I visit, imagining new ways to change

her behaviour. See, we're in Canada,
the Great White North—
where people take control,
who live with determined zest,
Controlling their destiny, too;
but she quickly laughs . . .
tells me to mind my manners,
finally.

ii
That night I imagine my mother skiing,
coming down a mountain with breakneck
speed as she loudly calls out to me—
and waves . . .
and tells me next what she's achieved.

But I see her tumble and fall,
then she's miraculously up again—
making dazzling turns, all her mark on
the prismatic Canadian soil—
          where else?
Who will doubt her zest?
Who can blame her for not trying hardest?
A gin and tonic next.

I mull over my words and feel guilty,
thinking I must leave her alone
with her memory intact, even as she
watches soap opera, day in and day out,
and all other acts on the TV
in the regular living room—
          in deepest silence.

My siblings, they mutter softly,
sometimes alone with her when I'm not
there, as she yet ponders going out
when the wind whistles,
the cold and the snow piling up—
she being outside with closed
eyes, furrowed brows . . .
                blinking next,
in perpetual sunlight.

HEMISPHERE OF LOVE

Into your bough body,
in the night's closet of years:
ancient voices at a standstill
as we call upon one another.

Seeds, offshoots, remembering
the veins that keep us going
with love, or suffused with blood,
semen of another place . . .

Do you always see the difference,
swimming underwater in a far sea?
The fruits we carry with us
are true vessels pouring out
as we cry with one voice,
with stranger acts ahead.

Locked in an embrace
and listening at this hour,
it's night's darkness that's all
in the white lining of clouds
bringing us closer because
of the one loud and long
 climactic song.

MICE AND MEN

Research scientists
at Cambridge
University
    say

A mother's genes
play a dominant
    role
in the development
of brain power

A father's genes
are much more likely
to shape a child's
emotional make-up
        and personality

Women wanting
intelligent and
well balanced
children
    need
not seek out
intellectual
    high-flyers

Men interested
in the IQ of their
children
should search for
        clever wives

Note: the study
so far
has only been
conducted
        on mice

FAGIN & ME

I encountered Fagin in a far place,
and asked, "You, what can you tell me?"

Imagining being Oliver Twist, and the book
I'd borrowed at the plantation library,

Read a dozen times over, and feared not
returning because of what the penalty might be.

So I talked to Mr Bumble, the beadle,
and Bill Sikes, Nancy, and Mr Brownlow;

But it was Fagin who remained with me
day after day, as voices kept calling out—

"Stop thief! Stop thief!"—still coming to me
in my sleep with sugar cane smells and molasses,

Amidst the factory's louder hum everywhere;
how I continued running, sweltering—

Heaving in, then trying to withstand
the Artful Dodger somewhere far from England.

Now it's without Dickens contemplating ease
in the tropics and still yearning for a place

Like an irksome pick-pocket crew, or experiencing
fear in my heart the more I continued to read

Loudly to myself, wanting to return to the library
with a kindhearted Mr Brownlow near me—

Sentimental or benevolent, or with the beadle
in a poorhouse—as someone kept wagging

A finger at me, Fagin in a London prison,
while I continued to sleep more fitfully.

THE VERY YOUNG

He tells an old story
of the war,
a life being snuffed out,
with longings of other days.

Amidst the young,
he's inclined to be
arrogant—
a mistaken breed, he avers.

They laugh after a while;
he, falling asleep . . .
then jolts back to attention,
with words harsh.

His tongue barbed, voice
raised louder. Finally
he says he always remembers
men whimpering in ditches,

The war still going on
in his head, as he walks about
in a circle:

As if they knew
it would be so from the beginning;
fitfully they laugh.

MY NEWLY ARRIVED
STUDENT FROM CHINA

Grain production in China
  is 62.2
million tons (of rice)
a year
  (400 kg per person:
population of China: 1.25 billion)

  Rice is planted
in more
than 20 provinces
in the south
  and southwest
(wheat in the north)

Historically China
  has suffered
from famine and threat
of hunger
  for a long time,
as my student, Kun Zhuo
    emphasizes,
  saying food shortage

  Hangs menacingly
over all the Chinese
  people's heads
like the sword of Damocles

  He praises agro-scientist
Yuan Longping, now 70,
at the Chinese Academy
  of Engineering

who's a leader specializing
in hybrid rice
                research

Yuan has won more awards
    than any scientist
        engaged in the study of atomic
and hydrogen bombs

        I smile, and say
quietly,
        I don't disagree
because of his being here
in Canada—
        all Kun's way of
        learning English
from a rice eater, too,
        like me.

OLYMPICS

The lady with the pistol
is ready to fire
broadsides
into the wind

here in the desert
empty shells
kick up their
heels
 and dance like
the invisible eagle—
arabesqued shadows
forming

At the hollow limits
of the ground.
And where the wind
skitters
another rows
with hands,
occasionally cupping
the waves. In this
water of life,
fish are hit

on their mouths—
as I try
to preserve songs
that are about
to become lost

same as the desire
for gold

(Los Angeles, 1984)

65

HE SPEAKS HIS LANGUAGE
(Found Poem: after Rosie DiManno)

Jasper Brown
is a little
bantam fellow.

Slim chest
thrust forward,
head ducking
and darting

As he speaks
his language—
an often incomprehensible
patois.

He communicates
in hand gestures,
abrupt movements,
arms flailing;

Knuckles rapping
against the edge of
the witness box—

Erupting now and then
in tiny spurts
of onomatopoeia—

Thereby better to describe
the screech
of a police car at his heels

Or the ruckus
he made the night
he was tossed into jail

For possession
of a substance
he knew damn well—

Wasn't crack cocaine.

I AM NOT

I am not West Indian,
I am not—
let me tell you again and again,
let Lamming and Selvon talk of places
        too distant from me
as I seethe and recover,
and shout with a false tongue
that I'm here—
nowhere else.

I conjure up other places,
cry out that all cities are the same:
rivers, seas, oceans . . .
as they swell or surrender
        at the same source.

        I breathe in the new soil,
        engorging myself with wind,
        yet flaccid;
inhaling the odour

of rice paddy,
cane leaves in the sun.

Birds blacker than the familiar vulture
circling my father's house—
                    amidst other voices
as I come to be with you,

Crying out
that there are hinterlands,
other terrain,
                    new boundaries,
and still I do not know.

I do not know—
in the cold, this heat
of the insides,
wetness at the corners of the mouth,
skin grown lighter.

And once the giant Lake Superior,
                    or foaminess of the Ottawa river . . .
Mohawk or Algonquin—
                    whither Carib or Arawak?

I breathe harder
                    with my many selves,
                    turning back—
looking at you only.

NEW ORLEANS VOODOO

My grandpa used
to say
something I never
forget, that
America is just
like a turkey,
it got white meat
and it got dark
meat; they is different
but they is both
important to the
turkey. I figure
the turkey
has more white
meat than dark
meat, but that
don't make any
difference. Both have
nerves running
through 'em.

THE POSTCOLONIALIST

The postcolonialist
seizes my brain
with wires.
I hardly know
what I'm about,
if to accept the other
or balk
at deconstruction

Committing myself
to familiar angst,
I succumb . . .
and let literary theorists
and philosophers—
Derrida or Foucault,
Bhaktin or Barthes—
have their say.

Being still or silent,
my senses intact,
the syllables of intellect
or the imagination
with rhythms arcane—
I aim only for the perfect line.

My muse's voice is yet quiet
as I take stock of memory,
a short cut to aesthetic enquiry—
distilling postmodernism
and then striking out with a hurrah
at this intellectual game
        or past-time discourse.

Now given to another country
without a European name,
I still consider origins,
muttering on about conquest
or simply pretending
with a buccaneer's quest,
chasing after silver and gold;
my words still salt-tongued,
it felt like, and being before
a wavering plank—
I step along with a nerve,
I've acquired, or with a determined will
all my own.

Yet theory will somehow
endure like hieroglyphs,
or last longer as I pretend
to answer questions about myself
with love or blandishment,
or what I've never known:
truths too magnanimous,
or still more precious—
though never really abstract.

I again balk at meaning
as emotions swirl,   and I say:
Let's pretend to make feelings real.
Do I outlast
the dross of critical theory?

MUSE

Promethean, i stand at the place of rock.
i bleed, and always i will answer with love,
the sun now a ball rolling away.

Icarus too i am,
this precious gift under my arms,
as i fly higher, meeting you eye to eye.

Tell me, winged horse, do i come close
to you, this last time, this moment,
when i will be inspired once again?

REWARDS

We need to remember the paradoxical
power in mutual vulnerability.
JOY KOGAWA

Bargaining with a higher power
to be really good to you,
as there are ways
to consider
the stages of grief.

First there's denial, then anger;
finally resignation,
 or simply haggling,
which is never good
        for the soul.

So you ask the self
to overlook disdain,
or make much ado
        about little
after being taken
for granted
        once again.

Narcissism is still all
with the power of words,
or being able to forgive
                another,
all that I take note of
with the self
        still in control.

ACKNOWLEDGEMENTS

Some of these poems originally appeared in:
ARIEL, Canadian Literature, Canadian Ethnic Studies, Canadian Housing, Caribbean Studies (University of Kentucky, US), *Descant, Drum* (University of Ottawa), *Kunapipi* (University of Wollongong, Australia), *Jouvert,* electronic (North Carolina State University), *The Ottawa Citizen, Small Axe* (University of Indiana), *The Toronto South Asian Review (*now *Toronto Review of Contemporary Writing),* and *World Literature Today* (University of Oklahoma).

"I Am Not" and "Multiculturalism" appeared in *Voices: Canadian Writers of African Descent,* ed. Ayanna Black (Harper and Collins, 1992; rpt. 2000). "Multiculturalism" also appeared in: *Symbiosis: An Intercultural Anthology of Poetry,* ed. L Diaz (Girol Books, 1992), *Breaking Free,* ed. J Borovilos (Prentice Hall,1994); *Insights:Cultures,* ed. J Terpening (Harcourt Brace Canada, 1995); *Making a Difference: Canadian Multicultural Literature,* ed. S Kambourelli (Oxford University Press, 1996); *Pens of Many Colours: A Canadian Reader,* eds. E Karpinski and I Lea (Harcourt, Brace & Co., 1996); *Fields of Vision: Readings in Culture, Race and Ethnicity,* ed. E Steig (Pearson Education Canada, 2001), and *Jouvert* (North Carolina State University, 2001).

"Gatineau Hills" appeared in *Six Ottawa Poets* (Mosaic Press, 1990), co-edited by Seymour Mayne. "Declaration," Horses in the Dark," and "My Mother" appeared in *Another Way to Dance: Contemporary Asian Poetry in Canada and the US* (TSAR, Toronto, 1996). "Mice and Men," in *Articulating Gender* (Pencraft International, India, 1999), and *Image,* Christmas special, ed. S Mayne, 2002. "For Rolf Hasenack" and "Acorn's Third World" appeared in *Symbiosis: An Intercultural Anthology of Poetry* (Ottawa: Girol Books, 1992).

Some of these poems were read on Carleton University Radio Station CKCU's *Third World Players Presents* hosted by Lloyd Stanford.

Thanks to the City of Ottawa, the Ontario Arts Council, and the Canada Council of the Arts for grants received. Some support may have been for previous projects, but which nevertheless allowed me time to work on some of these poems.

74